3

Wolf Moser

ls Canyon of the Snake River,
·th America's deepest gorge, forms
eastern border of Wallowa County.

Enjoying Wallowa County

In the extreme northeast corner of Oregon, bordering Washington and Idaho, lies Wallowa County, occupying 3,153 square miles, with a population of 7,250.

The majestic, rugged mountains tower nearly 10,000 feet above the gentle valleys where ranchers and loggers work. Deep canyons drop to the wild Imnaha and Snake rivers. Hells Canyon — the nation's deepest gorge — is here and draws thousands of visitors annually.

The county's divergent elevations encompass five life zones from Upper Sonoran (high desert) to Hudsonian alpine and sub-alpine zones.

Outdoor recreational activities are limitless. You can enjoy a gondola ride to the top of 8,256-foot Mt. Howard for hiking, viewing, picnicking and picture-taking.

Molly Murrill

Find a friend in the wilderness

Many visitors hike or backpack with horses or llamas into the Eagle Cap Wilderness from various trailheads or they venture into Hells Canyon via jet boat, kayak or raft.

Minam Lodge is not accessible by road, but a fly-in provides a spectacular view of the mountains and rivers. Hiking, horseback riding, fishing or just relaxing await you there.

Hoping for trout or steelhead, young and old cast their lines into rivers with such exotic names as Wallowa, Minam, Imnaha, Lostine, Grande Ronde and Snake or their tributaries, Hurricane Creek and Bear Creek. Wallowa Lake is a popular fishing and camping spot and a vacation destination in itself.

If you have the energy, you can fill every weekend in the summer. The list is long:

Chief Joseph Days and the Great Joseph Bank Robbery in Joseph, Mule Days in Enterprise, the huge Lostine Flea Market, Wallowa's Nez Perce Pow Wow and Friendship Feast and old-fashioned Fourth of July, the county fair, fireworks over Wallowa Lake, arts festivals for both adults and youth entrants, an old-time fiddlers' competition, small airplane fly-ins, and the Oregon Mountain Cruise classic car rally.

Several music festivals, concerts, theatrical productions, along with two annual writers' conferences, draw attendees from near and far. Other folks visit the numerous art galleries and bronze foundries.

Herds of deer and elk bring hunters from a wide range. A few are lucky enough to get a once-in-a-lifetime tag for bighorn sheep and mountain goat. You may choose a guide or outfitter for your wilderness or fishing trip.

In fall and winter, events include the Bavarian Alpenfest at Wallowa Lake and the handcrafters' Christmas bazaars in Wallowa and Enterprise.

Powder snow makes Ferguson Ridge, east of Joseph, Wallowa County's main downhill ski area. Cross-country skiing is excellent, with Nordic shelters for those on long treks.

Another popular winter sport is snowmobiling, especially from Salt Creek Summit over to the rim of Hells Canyon.

Viewing the fantastic scenery, you can see why the county is called the Switzerland of America. Photo opportunities leap from every corner and unlimited activities are yours to experience each season of the year.

4

ABOVE: This photo taken by historian J.H. Horner depicts the reburial of Old Chief Joseph from near the confluence of the Wallowa and Lostine Rivers to the shores of Wallowa Lake on Sept. 26, 1926. At left is Joe Albert (Elaskolatat). Chief McFarland holds the horse which pulled the traverse that carried the old chief's body. (Photo courtsey Wallowa County Museum)

RIGHT: A huge parachute provides the cover for dancers at the annual Pow Wow which has helped bring the Nez Perce and whites together in recent years.

Ray Linker

Native Americans played a big role in early history

Original dwellers of the Wallowa Valley, the Nez Perce Indians, or Nee Me Poo (We, the People), were forced out by land-hungry pioneers in the 1870s. The Nez Perce War of 1877 saw the Indians pursued by Army troops through Idaho, Wyoming and Montana for 1,700 miles before their surrender within 30 miles of Canada at Bear Paw Mountain. The Indians were moved to midwestern reservations, where many died from disease. In 1885 the remaining 268 returned to the Northwest, 118 to Lapwai and 150 to the Colville Reservation at Nespelem, Wash. The Joseph Band remains on the Colville reservation today.

Old Chief Joseph (Tuekakas) died in 1870 and is buried at Wallowa Lake. His son, Young Chief Joseph, known as Hin-Ma-To-Yoh-La-Kit, led the 1877 retreat against the whites. He died in 1904 and is buried in Nespelam.

Today, Wallowa County citizens and the Nez Perce plan a Nez Perce Trail Interpretive Center on 160 acres near Wallowa. The site will include an outdoor campground, where the tribe can provide cultural and heritage training to youth and a permanent site for the Pow Wow and Friendship Feast. — *Ray Linker*

Steelhead, trout and chinook lure fishermen to Wallowa County's streams and rivers.

Frances Buckl

Wallowa, population 805, offers varied architecture along its main street.

Wolf Mos

With a population of only 220, Lostine residents enjoy the old-fashioned coziness of their town.

Wolf Moser

The Wallowa County-Nez Perce Salmon Recovery Plan has become a model for other areas.

Wolf Moser

8 The Grande Ronde River winds through Troy toward the Snake River.

Wolf Mose

Ray Link

North Country

The north end of Wallowa County has several attractive features. The Grande Ronde and Wenaha rivers converge at Troy, a hot spot for fishermen. Hunters come to try their luck with the abundant wild game, such as bighorn sheep, bear, cougar, deer, elk, chukar, turkey and grouse.

The canyon benches of the Troy and Flora area support wheat, sheep and cattle.

Once flourishing Flora now has only a few residents. Some folks still ride their horses for miles to pick up their books at the Flora branch of the county library.

Visitors also will enjoy nearby Joseph Canyon.

Wolf Moser

Linda Eytchison

Volunteers operate the Wallowa County Museum in Joseph between May and September.

Linda Eytchison

Located in the heart of Enterprise, this historic courthouse is the seat of county government.

Linda Eytchison

Enterprise, with a population of 2,020, provides retail shopping, dining and theater.

Wolf Moser

Hells Canyon Mule Days and parade in Enterprise bring entrants from several states.

Linda Eytchison

12

The majestic Wallowa Mountains form the backdrop for the village of Joseph, home to several fine arts bronze foundries and numerous galleries. Enterprise and Wallowa also have foundries. Events include the summer Great Joseph Bank Robbery enactment; Oregon Mountain Cruise in June. Chief Joseph Days Rodeo, parade and Nez Perce Friendship Feast are always the last full weekend in July.

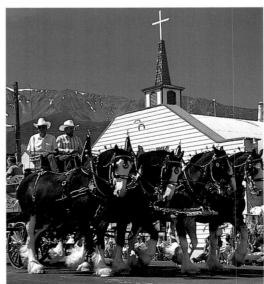

14

With the lake far below, the Wallowa Lake Tramway glides to the top of 8,256-foot high Mt. Howard. It is the steepest and longest vertical lift for a four-passenger gondola in North America. The view is unsurpassed and there are more than two miles of hiking trails on top.

September's Alpenfest at Wallowa Lake has singing, dancing, lots of good food and booths with a wide variety of arts and crafts.

The Fourth of July wouldn't be complete without taking in the fireworks over Wallowa Lake.

A summertime hiker pauses in the Eagle Cap Wilderness. Only horse trails and a good dirt airstrip provide access to remote Minam Lodge, where horses get extensive use by guests.

Alan Klages

Ray Linker

Cattle huddle as ranchers round them up for spring branding in the Imnaha canyon country.

Wolf Moser

This small building opposite the tavern/store is all the Post Office needs to get the mail out.

Linda Eytchison

Marilyn Goebel

In the Clover

The little unincorporated town of Imnaha, with its quaint buildings, is a gathering place for ranchers from miles around.

Cattle industry provides economic stability.

The dark-colored morel mushrooms are harvested in spring by people from all over the northwest.

The largehead red clover is found at various elevations. These are growing high in the Hells Canyon Wilderness.

Eric Valentine

18

Mt. Howard
Elev. 8,256

Aneroid
Elev. 9,702

Bonneville
Elev. 8,902

Chief Joseph Mt
Elev. 9,617

East Moraine

West Moraine

WALLOWA LAKE (Formed by glacial drift) 285 ft. deep

Hunters' Delight

An abundance of wildlife is a big drawing card for hunters.

Getting a permit to go after Rocky Mountain Bighorn Sheep is a once-in-a-lifetime experience. The bighorns roam the Lostine Canyon and Hells Canyon.

Hunters also seek out chukar, grouse, turkeys, geese and duck.

Black bears are found in several locations of the county.

Elk have a large range throughout Wallowa County. Both rifle and archery hunting are popular.

Troy hosts an annual rendezvous for muzzle-loaders.

Eric Valentine

19

Jane Rohling

Alan Klages

Linda Casady

Twin Peaks
Elev. 9,673

Sawtooth
Elev. 9,174

Ruby Peak
Elev. 8,874

© CHUCK GARRE
Copyright Chuck Garrett

Doris Woempner

Ray Linker

It's all in the point of view

The vistas of the wide open canyon country make traveling to Dug Bar, Buckhorn Springs, Snake River or Hat Point enjoyable. Kayaking and rafting the white waters of the Snake River are popular.

Kim Lamb

21

Linda Eytchison

Eric Valentine   Eric Valentine

Marilyn Goebe

Outdoors in the Wallowas can produce a variety of experiences. Llamas are easy on vegetation and
sometimes-fragile trails in the Eagle Cap Wilderness. Skookum Ridge and Falls Creek Falls in the
Wallowa-Whitman National Forest are attractions to many hikers. Horses are one means of access to
campsites and fishing in remote areas. The highest fishable lake in Oregon is Legore Lake at 8,800 feet

Doris Woempner

Linda Etychison

23

Cheryl Crawley

Alan Klag

A winter wonderland makes snowmobiling and skiing favorite sports of residents and visitors. When Wallowa Lake freezes, ice hockey, as well as skating and ice fishing, are attractions for all ages.

Kim Lamb

Wallowa County Arts

Wallowa County provides artists and artisans with unlimited opportunities. The pouring of molten bronze in one of the several fine arts foundries in the county casts a glow on the workers. Most foundries offer tours to the public. One of the various cottage industries is glassblowing. Self-employment makes up 22 percent of the workforce. That figure is the second highest among all counties in the state. Diverse products are leather goods, artwork and Indian artifact replicas. The public art display in front of the Joseph Post Office is one of several on view along Main Street in both Enterprise and Joseph.

Wolf Moser

Fall colors of tamarack stand out among other trees in the forest. Timber is strong in Wallowa County despite the decline of harvests from U.S. Forest Service lands. Both large and small companies are making efforts to diversify to find new markets, including those for secondary wood products. Sustainable Northwest, an innovative non-profit group interested in keeping a healthy environment and family-wage jobs, has been working with a local group, Wallowa Resources.

saw-filer keeps Wallowa County sawmills on the cutting edge of the timber industry.

Alan Kla...

Productive Ranches & Farms

Canola, winter wheat, barley, potatoes, alfalfa and mixed hays are some of Wallowa County's agricultural products. Bunch grasses provide rich grazing for livestock and wild game.

Alan Klages

Eric Valen...

Mt. Howard is a jumping-off place for paragliders. Patchwork design of farms forms the backdrop. *Molly Murrill*

typical farm scene near Lostine is complete with a tractor, dogs and a familiar old round barn. *Linda Eytchison*

Historically, the cattle industry has played a large part in the economy of Wallowa County.

Wolf Mos

Wolf Mo

Ray Linker

Wallowa County Search and Rescue Unit members prepare to launch a mission from the Enterprise Municipal Airport, with an assist from the Oregon National Guard. Joseph State Airport, with its 5,200-foot-long runway can accommodate jets weighing up to 12,500 pounds.

Ray Linker

Helpful facts about Wallowa County

Wallowa County has no stop lights or parking meters. People know their neighbors, and the world moves at a slower place.

Want to visit or move to this community in the northeast corner of Oregon? Here is information you may find helpful.

Economy

Wallowa County's economy is driven by ranching, farming, timber and wood products, arts, tourism, and retail.

Farms range in size from five acres to large ranches, many with cattle or sheep. Harvesting or producing timber and other wood products keeps others busy. The fine arts industry, which includes several bronze-casting foundries as well as studios and galleries, also provides jobs.

The economy is becoming more diversified, with telecommunications spawning home-based businesses. Other cottage industries include those that produce secondary wood products.

The U.S. Forest Service and school districts account for a sizeable amount of the employment in Wallowa County.

A motel-restaurant-convention center in Enterprise is the latest addition to the amenities for visitors. Other motels and bed-and-breakfasts offer more than 200 rooms and camping is available in federal, state and private campgrounds.

The county is reaching out to retired people. Condos and a retirement complex will be built in the near future.

Restaurants abound in the area.

Film and video production companies have been active here, beginning with the "Winds of Chance" in 1927. More recent films have included "Homeward Bound, the Incredible Journey," "500 Nations," a Kevin Costner production and Ken Burns' "The West." Commericals have also been filmed in the county.

Utilities

Electric service: Pacific Power and Light Co. Telephone service: GTE Northwest Inc. , U.S. Cellular and Cellular One.

Communications

The county is served by KWVR radio at 1340 AM and 92.1 FM. Crestview Cable TV provides 34 channels, with time and weather plus FM radio stations. The Wallowa County Chieftain is a weekly newspaper in Enterprise. The La Grande Observer is a daily newspaper circulating in Wallowa County. Several companies provide access to the internet.

Government

Enterprise is the county seat. The county is governed by a County Court, headed by an administrative judge with no judicial powers. The cities of Enterprise, Joseph, Lostine and Wallowa are governed by elected city councils and mayors.

Medical Care

Wallowa Memorial Hospital is a modern 32-bed hospital which has a maternity ward, a four-bed intensive care unit and a coronary care unit, eight medical doctors and 24-hour, seven-day-a-week emergency room service. Air transportation to large medical centers for specialized patient care is from the Joseph State Airport. Wallowa County has an active, well-trained, state certified volunteer search and rescue unit.

A nursing home, county health department, mental health center, assisted-living facility and several adult foster homes tend to other special needs. Four dentists and one dental lab serve residents.

Education

The county offers pre-school and K-12 classes in each community. Adult education is available. Off-campus classes are offered through Eastern Oregon State College of La Grande and Blue Mountain Community College of Pendleton. Both have offices in Enterprise. Some classes are taught through Ed-Net facilities, offering group communication with both visual and voice transmissions between students and instructors.

Weather

High mountains protect the valley from the most severe aspects of storms that cross the area. Both temperature and precipitation vary with elevation. The average maximum temperature for July is 84. The average minimum low in January is 14. The precipitation is 18.85 inches per year.

Photo Club is going strong

Started in 1988, the non-profit Wallowa Valley Photo Club annually produces a scenic calendar of Wallowa County which has drawn wide acclaim and sells worldwide. Our calendar and members' dues are the only means of raising funds for projects. The club holds annual exhibits for members, assists with the exhibits by adults and youth at the county fair, awards scholarships for youngsters to attend classes and seminars and gives slide presentations to groups. Members have been published in a variety of trade journals, magazines, books, and newspapers. Club membership is diverse, including a judge, writers, ranchers, housewives, business people and retirees. Their photographic abilities have a wide range, and the club is always seeking new members!

Eric Valentine

Many enjoy hiking to Boy Scout Falls near the head of Wallowa Lake and the Scouting complex.

Clubs and organizations

Wallowa County offers many clubs and organizations, including Rotary, Elks, Lions, IOOF, American Legion, Wallowa Valley Arts Council, AARP, Masons, Veterans of Foreign Wars, Scouting, Campfire, Good Sams, Granges, Wallowa Valley Photo Club, Ferguson Ski Club, snowmobilers, fiddlers, quilters, 4-H, FFA, FBLA, FFCL, Beta Nu, Beta Sigma Phi, Soroptomists, sports booster clubs, drama groups. Most religious denominations are represented.

Contributing Sponsors

This book is made possible in part by contributions from the following sponsors:

- Sustainable Northwest
- The City of Enterprise
- The City of Lostine
- The City of Wallowa
- The Joseph Chamber of Commerce/Chief Joseph Days Rodeo
- Enterprise Merchants Association
- Joseph Merchants Association
- Valley Bronze of Oregon Inc. and Fine Art Bronze Gallery
- The Bank of Wallowa County
- Arnold Fredricks/WF Development Inc.
- Hubbard Ranch/Joe Collins
- Parmenter Studio and The Summerhouse Gallery
- The Manuel Museum, David and Lee Manuel
- Alpine Insurance Co./Steve Zollman
- Eric Valentine
- The Bookloft/Book Corner
- Parks Bronze
- Bronze Gallery of Joseph
- Moffit Brothers Transportation
- Pacific Power
- GTE Northwest Inc.
- U.S. Forest Service
- The La Grande Observer
- Wildhorse Gallery
- Wallowa County Board of Realtors
- Wallowa County Chieftain
- Wallowa County
- Wallowa County Health Care District
- Wallowa Forest Products
- Wallowa County Chamber of Commerce
- Wallowa Valley Arts Council
- Doris Woempner

35

WALLOWA VALLEY

Photo Club

Published by S.A.P. — Slap and Paste Publishing Co.,
P.O. Box 1050, Joseph, OR 97846.
Printed in the U.S.A.
For additional copies of this book,
contact the Wallowa Valley Photo Club.

ISBN 0-9656831-0-9

$9.95

50995

9 780965 683104